PICCADILLO'S CORNISH ADVENTURE

A TRUE STORY

WRITTEN AND ILLUSTRATED BY ANTHEA HOWELL

PAVO PRESS

All rights reserved; no part of this publication may be reproduced or transmitted by any means without the prior permission of the publisher.
This edition 2002. Pavo Press, PO Box No.78, Liskeard, Cornwall. PL14 5WA.

Copyright © Anthea Howell 2001.

The moral right of the author has been asserted.

ISBN 0 9542 5570 4 – Limp edition.

ISBN 09542 5571 2 – Cased edition.

Printed and Bound by Short Run Press Ltd, Exeter

PICCADILLO'S CORNISH ADVENTURE

Something strange was about to happen!

The little puffin was used to storms. There was no shelter in the vast loneliness of the cold North Sea. He could ride the wildest waves or dive below the surface to escape for a while. Storms soon passed.

Today, the very air felt different. He could sense that something new - something evil - was heading towards him.

For a while, the little puffin carried on as usual, sometimes bobbing about on the surface, sometimes diving deep, deep down after fish, twisting and turning, using his stubby little wings like paddles to propel him through the water. He could not shake off the bad feeling, though.

His strong little wings lifted him high above the rising waves. He began flying fast, towards the south-west, speeding away from the horror, which seemed just behind him.

And then it caught up with him!

A howling, screaming horror, a wind like an evil demon, it tossed and buffeted him, sometimes catching him up, sometimes pitching him down into the waves, but ever driving him on.

Hours passed. The light faded, but still there was no rest for the weary little bird.

Suddenly he was aware of lights ahead. They were not stars. They twinkled, but they were too low for stars.

A sheer wall, like the face of a cliff, loomed up at him. Somehow he made his tired wings lift him up to clear the obstacle. He crashed down on to a very hard surface and knew no more.

In the pale light of a January dawn, traffic was beginning to build up on the London bridge. A few early - rising pedestrians hurried along the pavement. No-one had time to notice the little bundle of feathers lying squashed against the wall.

It was much later that the little puffin was spotted by two children on their way to school. At first, Adam and Jessica were sure the bird was dead, but when Adam carefully picked it up, they saw a faint flicker, as the little puffin tried to open its eyes.

"We must take it to the R.S.P.C.A. I know where it is. It's in Jermyn Street," said Jessica.

The little puffin was far too exhausted to know what was happening to him during the next few hours. His arrival at the R.S.P.C.A. Headquarters had caused quite a stir. No-one could remember having seen a wild puffin in London before.

When the little puffin finally opened his eyes, he thought at first he was still in the heart of the storm. There was a loud noise and he could sense that he was moving. He realised that he was safe and comfortable, and still so very tired, and was soon fast asleep.

He slept on, as his basket was moved from the train to a van and then into the Wild Bird Hospital, in the village of Mousehole in Cornwall.

The puffin was too weak to struggle when a strange creature took hold of him. For a moment, he thought he was a chick again, as his beak was opened and fishy oil went down his throat. Then he was left alone, in a warm and cosy place.

Dorothy and her sister, Phyllis (always known as Pog) stood watching for a while, until they were satisfied all was well with the latest arrival. This was not the first puffin to be helped at their Wild Bird Hospital, but the others had been found on the nearby Cornish beaches.

"We'll call him Piccadillo, as he was found in London," decided Dorothy.

Piccadillo gradually grew stronger during that first week. Two other puffins had also been found in London and brought down by train to Cornwall. The sisters had named them Kontiki and The Small World.

Soon they were fit enough to be allowed to come into the sitting-room in the evenings. They were put on the couch to get some exercise, but Piccadillo soon got bored with this. He found that it was fun to jump from the couch across to the arm of the chair and back, and even jumped up on the shade of the table lamp!

Piccadillo seemed to know that the strange human creatures were friendly, and when he was introduced to yet another strange creature - Dusky the Collie dog - he took to him as well.

He would sit on a cushion next to Dusky on the couch, or even on Dusky's warm back.

Dorothy and Pog were very kind ladies. Every day, they would prepare their own bath for the puffins to use.

First they put in a rock, on a soft cover so as not to scratch the bath. Sometimes they only half-filled the bath with water, but the puffins preferred to dive, not paddle, so they liked the bath filled to the brim.

Piccadillo and Kontiki particularly enjoyed the daily swim. They made an awful mess on the bathroom floor!

The three puffins were now well enough to leave the comfort of the house. Wild birds were only kept until they could be set free again. Piccadillo, Kontiki and The Small World must get used gradually to life in their natural habitat.

They were put in one of the outside sheds, which had a wire-netting run with an outside pool.

Piccadillo had been carried in a box many times now. Each time the box was opened, something new was to be seen, but this time was very different.

The wet rocks were rough under his feet. Salty spray splashed up, soaking his feathers. His little heart began to beat faster and faster, as he realised what was in front of him. There was no wall or wire fence to hold him in. There before him was just the glory of the open sea, with his puffin friends waiting for him to lead them!

He flapped his wings to test them. Then, without a backward look, he took off, his little wings working furiously until he gained height. He soared over the waves and was soon no longer to be seen.

Dorothy and Phyllis stood for a while watching, until the three little puffins were out of sight.

Although there was always a certain thrill in setting wild birds free, there was sadness too.

They would never forget Piccadillo and the other two puffins, but other birds were waiting for them.

They turned to go back. The work must go on.

The Wild Bird Hospital was founded in 1928 by the Misses Dorothy and Phyllis Yglesias. Over the years the Sanctuary has become famous, especially so during the Torrey Canyon disaster, when over 8,000 oiled birds passed through the hospital.

In 1953, the R.S.P.C.A. took over the massive task of running the Hospital, but in 1975 they were forced by monetary difficulties to decide to close it.

After a public appeal and, later, a Public Meeting, a Committee was selected to run the Hospital on the same lines as before. In July, 1976, the Sanctuary became a charity in its own right.

Sadly, the two sisters have since died, Pog in 1977 and Dorothy in 1980 (a month after she received the M.B.E. in the Queen's Honours List), but the work goes on.